BATTLEFIELDS ACROSS AMERICA

NEW ORLEANS

DAVID C. KING

Twenty-First Century Books

Brookfield, Connecticut

Twenty-First Century Books
A Division of The Millbrook Press
2 Old New Milford Road
Brookfield, CT 06804

Printed in the United States of America on acid free paper ∞.

Created and produced in association with Blackbirch Graphics, Inc.

Photo Credits
Cover: Fort McHenry National Monument, National Park Service; pages 4, 7, 8, 9, 11, 13, 15, 16, 18, 21, 22, 27, 30, 33, 34, 43, 46: North Wind Pictures; page 17: Blackbirch Press, Inc.; page 24: Library of Congress; pages 28, 52, 55: Eastern National; pages 50, 56: Fort McHenry National Monument, National Park Service; page 54: Jean Lafitte National Historical Park and Preserve.

All maps by Bob Italiano/©Blackbirch Graphics, Inc.

Library of Congress Cataloging-in-Publication Data

King, David C.
  New Orleans / David C. King.
      p.   cm. — (Battlefields across America)
  Includes bibliographical references and index.
  Summary: Focuses on the final battle of the War of 1812, which actually took place after the war ended, describes it in the context of the entire conflict, and examines related sites that can be visited today.
    ISBN 0-7613-3010-0 (lib bdg. : alk. paper)
    1. New Orleans (La.), Battle of, 1815—Juvenile literature. [1. New Orleans (La.), Battle of, 1815. 2. United States—History—War of 1812—Campaigns.] I. Title. II. Series.
E356.N5K56   1998
973.5'239—dc21
                                                                97-51203
                                                                    CIP
                                                                     AC

CONTENTS

THE WAR OF 1812:
THE SECOND WAR FOR INDEPENDENCE

In the early 1800s, the United States found itself caught in the middle of the tremendous European power struggle known as the Napoleonic Wars. In these wars, Great Britain was attempting to stop the French emperor, Napoleon, from conquering all of Europe. Both sides were demanding that the United States stop trading with the other.

American trade ships were seized by both the French and British and their cargo was confiscated. Only two decades after winning their independence from Great Britain, Americans had to decide how they would meet this new challenge.

The young American republic depended heavily on trade with Europe. Western farmers sent products like wheat and corn, while Southerners shipped cotton to the mills of England and other countries. People in the Northeast exported lumber, ships, and some farm products. In exchange, Americans bought European manufactured goods, such as clothing, tools, and machinery, as well as products from European colonies, including sugar, coffee, tea, and spices. Because of this dependence on Europe, farmers, manufacturers, and merchants were all hurt by the British and French interference with American ships.

To make matters worse, the French often seized the ship as well as the cargo, although they always freed the crew. The British, in need of seamen, frequently took American sailors off the seized vessel and "impressed" them, or forced them into service on British ships. As one American congressman wrote, "The Devil himself cannot tell which government, Britain or France, is the most wicked."[1]

< 5 >

< 6 >

"Free Trade and Sailors' Rights"

The dispute over the interference with American shipping slowly grew more heated between 1803 and 1812. The United States, as a neutral nation, insisted on its rights to trade anywhere it wished. But the British and French simply ignored the Americans' position, which was summed up by the popular slogan "Free Trade and Sailors' Rights."

President Thomas Jefferson and Congress tried to end the conflict by placing an embargo, or ban, on all trade with Europe in December 1807. In March 1808, Congress passed the Non-Intercourse Act, which limited the embargo, preventing trade only with France and Great Britain. Since America was a major market for French and English goods, the Americans hoped that the economic pressure of an embargo would force Great Britain and France to stop disrupting American trade. In the end, the embargo was a failure. The people it hurt the most turned out to be the American farmers and merchants who depended heavily on trade with both France and Great Britain.

When James Madison became president in 1809, he persuaded Congress to try a new policy. The United States would renew trade with England and France, but if either country agreed to end its interference with American ships, the United States would immediately stop all trade with the other. Napoleon quickly agreed to leave American ships alone (although secretly, he ordered his warships to continue seizing American cargoes). Napoleon's agreement to stop harassing the Americans in word, if not deed, led to an American embargo of trade with Great Britain. The British held out, refusing to let American ships pass freely, even though the lack of American trade was causing economic havoc throughout the British Isles.

< 7 >

America's "War Hawks"

War fever had been steadily building in the United States since June 22, 1807, when a British warship shelled the American ship *Chesapeake*, killing 21 men and impressing 4 sailors. Agitation for war did not come from the shipowners and merchants of New

The shelling of the Chesapeake *by a British warship increased the American public's desire to go to war.*

< 8 >

Henry Clay

England, however, but rather from the South and the new states of the West. A group of Republican congressmen, led by Henry Clay of Kentucky, were so insistent in their call for war against Great Britain that they became known as the "War Hawks."

Clay and the War Hawks were convinced that the nation's pride and honor were at stake. They were also very interested in expanding the boundaries of the United States, and they thought that war might give Americans a chance to conquer British Canada and the Floridas, controlled at this time by Great Britain's ally, Spain.

An incident on the northwestern frontier strengthened the War Hawks' demands for war. American settlers moving west were constantly pushing into Indian lands. The Indians began raiding white settlements, and different tribes came together to fight for their land and resist westward expansion. In November 1811, a militia army in the Indiana Territory fought an alliance of Native American tribes united by the brilliant Shawnee chief named Tecumseh. At the battle of Tippecanoe, Tecumseh's warriors were forced to retreat. The weapons and supplies they left behind were British, and this convinced many Americans that the British were plotting with Tecumseh to conquer the American Northwest.

As the war fever increased, and the British showed no signs of ending their capture of American ships, President Madison became

< 9 >

convinced that war was the only answer. Unknown to Madison, the British government had decided to end its interference with American shipping. But that decision came too late. On June 16, 1812, with the agreement of a majority of Congress, Madison officially declared war against Great Britain.

Indians, led by Tecumseh, were soundly defeated by American forces at the battle of Tippecanoe.

Even those who fought against the Shawnee chief Tecumseh were impressed by his courageous and powerful leadership. His greatest adversary, William Henry Harrison, governor of the Indiana Territory, wrote: "The implicit obedience and respect which followers of Tecumseh pay him is really astonishing and… bespeaks him one of those uncommon geniuses which spring up occasionally to produce revolutions and overturn the established order of things."[2]

Between 1800 and 1813, as many as 100,000 white settlers had pushed into Indian lands in western Georgia, Spanish Florida, and present-day Alabama and Mississippi. Tecumseh, also called Crouching Panther, had a vision of uniting all the tribes east of the Mississippi River, creating a force powerful enough to drive the Americans back to the Atlantic coast.

With his brother Tenskwatawa, known as the Prophet, Tecumseh managed to persuade several thousand people from different tribes to join him. The two brothers established a settlement called Prophetstown on the Tippecanoe River in present-day Indiana—part of the Shawnee territory, which stretched from Kentucky to Indiana.

Beginning in 1809, Tecumseh made several trips south, hoping to persuade more tribes, especially the powerful Creek nation, to join him. An American militia officer who heard one of his speeches wrote that "His eyes burned with supernatural lustre…[and] his voice resounded over the multitude…hurling out his words like a succession of thunderbolts."[3]

In November 1811, while Tecumseh was on one of these journeys, Harrison led a militia army into Prophetstown. Tenskwatawa foolishly disobeyed his brother's orders not to fight. The Indians were routed at what became known as the battle of Tippecanoe. Tecumseh returned to find his town in ashes. "I swore once more eternal hatred," he said, "the hatred of an avenger."[4] With his hopes for an Indian confederacy shattered, Tecumseh joined forces with the British in the War of 1812.

William Henry Harrison (right) and Tecumseh were on opposite sides in the conflict caused by the westward expansion of white settlers into Indian territory.

On October 5, 1813, Harrison's American force defeated the British and Tecumseh's braves in the battle of the Thames. The man who claimed to fire the shot that killed Tecumseh, Colonel Richard M. Johnson, later became vice-president under Martin Van Buren. And, 30 years after the battle, Harrison, the "hero of Tippecanoe," was elected president.

< 12 >

For the War Hawks, this was to be "the Second War for American Independence." But in New England and other parts of the Northeast, members of the Federalist party remained staunchly opposed to the war.

"Mr. Madison's War"

The United States was totally unprepared for war. The army had fewer than 10,000 men, and few civilians were interested in enlisting. The navy had several outstanding commanders, but only a handful of ships. The treasury had scant funds for war, and the government's efforts to raise money by selling war bonds were not very successful.

Most damaging of all was the lack of national unity. The Federalists labeled the conflict "Mr. Madison's War," and even resisted the government's request for state militia forces. The year 1812 was an election year, and Madison did manage to win a second term, but the Federalists carried every northern state except Vermont and Pennsylvania.

From the beginning, the land war was almost a complete disaster for the United States. American army and militia forces tried to attack the British in the closest place they could be reached— Canada. But the poorly trained militiamen rarely fought well, and there were not enough volunteers. Many Americans mistakenly believed that entering the foreign soil of Canada somehow made them part of the regular U.S. Army, and therefore, committed to five years of service. The overly cautious leadership of the American generals, many of them aging veterans of the Revolutionary War, also contributed to the military weakness of the United States. As a result of all these factors, efforts to invade Canada by way of Detroit, the Niagara River and Lake Champlain all failed.

< 13 >

There were a few bright spots, however, in the war against Great Britain. The small U.S. Navy distinguished itself in several one-on-one battles against British men-of-war. The pride of the U.S. fleet, the *Constitution*, won dramatic victories in 1812 and earned the nickname "Old Ironsides" when British cannonballs failed to penetrate the ship's thick oak hull. On September 10, 1813, in the battle of Lake Erie, Captain Oliver Hazard Perry, commanding ten hastily built ships, destroyed a British squadron. Not only did the battle end British control of Lake Erie, but the victory, and Perry's

The American ship Constitution *won many naval victories for the United States, including this one against the British ship* Guerrière.

< 14 >

terse and now famous message—"We have met the enemy and they are ours!"[5]—were a boost to the nation's sagging morale. An American fleet, however small, had defeated a fleet of the world's greatest navy. In Congress, War Hawk John C. Calhoun crowed, "The charm of British naval invincibility is broken."[6]

A few weeks later, William Henry Harrison led a militia force in one of the few successful invasions of Canada. At the battle of the Thames, on October 5, 1813, Harrison's troops routed a combined British and Native American force. The great Indian leader Tecumseh was killed, ending his dream of uniting the tribes against the wave of American settlers advancing west over the Appalachian Mountains.

1814: A Year of Disaster

The British had no intention of yielding their naval superiority to the Americans. By late 1813, the Royal Navy had committed enough ships to the western Atlantic to blockade the coast of the United States. Although American privateers—armed merchant ships that were licensed to capture enemy cargo vessels—managed to elude the blockade, the American warships were trapped in their harbors.

In April 1814, the British and their allies finally defeated France and forced Napoleon to give up his position as Emperor of France. Great Britain could now concentrate its energies, including thousands of battle-hardened soldiers, on its campaign against the United States. The British navy began ranging up and down the American coast, landing parties of soldiers and marines who raided towns from Maine to Georgia. Great Britain even annexed part of Maine.

By the late summer of 1814, a large British force was ready to invade the United States from Canada by way of Lake Champlain. At the same time, a powerful British fleet further south sailed

Having successfully blockaded American ships in their harbors, the British navy traveled up the Chesapeake to land soldiers in Maryland in 1814.

into Chesapeake Bay and landed an army on the coast of Maryland. On August 24, a hastily assembled American militia force faced British soldiers briefly at Bladensburg, Maryland, but fled as soon as the shooting started.

The President's House is Set Afire

After the encounter at Bladensburg, the British landing force marched into Washington, D.C., without further opposition. From what was then called the "President's House," Dolley Madison, wife

Facing almost no resistance, British troops marched into Washington, D.C., on August 24, 1814, and set fire to many government buildings, including the President's House.

of the president, had heard the cannons being fired at Bladensburg. With a telescope, she watched "groups of [American] military wandering in all directions as if there was a lack of arms or of spirit to fight for their own fireside."[7] Mrs. Madison managed to escape with little more than a famous portrait of George Washington, which she had vowed to protect.

After enjoying the dinner that had been set out but abandoned in the President's House, the British set the building ablaze, then

< 17 >

torched the Capitol and several other government buildings. A fierce thunderstorm prevented further damage. The British set off next for Baltimore, while the saddened citizens of Washington, including the president, crept back to their charred capital. A British newspaper predicted that within a year, all major American cities would be "heaps of smoldering rubbish."[9]

The Americans Keep Fort McHenry

In Baltimore, the British encountered a more determined defense by the Americans. For 25 hours on September 12 and 13, the British navy bombarded Fort McHenry, which guarded the city, and tried to land an assault force. But they failed to do much damage, and Admiral Sir Alexander Cochrane ordered a withdrawal. During the night, a young attorney named Francis Scott Key was onboard a British warship arranging a prisoner exchange. Watching the tattered

American forces were able to withstand the British bombardment of Fort McHenry in September 1814.

A year before the British bombardment of Fort McHenry, the fort's commander, Major George Armistead, requested a flag for the fort, "a flag so large that the British will have no difficulty seeing it at a distance."[8] The task of making the flag fell to a widow, Mary Young Pickersgill, a professional flag maker. Mrs. Pickersgill made a big flag—each of the 15 stars measured 2 feet across, and the whole flag required 400 yards of material.

During the British attack, Francis Scott Key, a lawyer, was on a British warship arranging the release of a prisoner. Key was held overnight so that he would not reveal the British plans for a land attack. Throughout the night, Key looked through a spyglass (a small telescope) to make sure that Mrs. Pickersgill's flag still flew above the fort, which was illuminated by the explosion of bombs and the red glare of rockets.

As dawn broke over the harbor, and the flag still fluttered defiantly, Key scribbled the opening lines of a poem on an envelope he had in his

Francis Scott Key

American flag continue to fly above the fort inspired Key to write the first lines of a poem that became the "Star-Spangled Banner."

The day before the British tried to take Fort McHenry, an American naval squadron on Lake Champlain won a surprising victory over a British fleet. The battle of Lake Champlain ended, at least for the moment, the danger of a British invasion from Canada. Having failed to subdue Fort McHenry, Admiral Cochrane directed Great Britain's Atlantic fleet south to the Caribbean Sea.

pocket. He finished the poem the next day onshore. Key decided to set the poem to music, and for the melody, he chose a song called "To Anacreon in Heaven." (Anacreon was a poet in ancient Greece.) Ironically, this tune was of British origin.

Key showed the poem to friends, and one took it to a Baltimore newspaper office, where it was printed as a broadside, or leaflet, with the title, "Defence of Fort M'Henry." Within weeks, Key's song had become immensely popular throughout the country. It was given the new title of "The Star-Spangled Banner." The stirring words seemed to capture perfectly the suspense of that dramatic night and the tremendous relief Americans felt when Fort McHenry held firm.

Throughout the nineteenth century, "The Star-Spangled Banner" was a kind of unofficial national anthem, played on every patriotic occasion. The U.S. Navy adopted the song as its official anthem in 1889, and the Army followed in 1903. In 1931, Congress voted to make "The Star-Spangled Banner" the official national anthem, although some critics argued that the melody was too difficult to sing. As for Mrs. Pickersgill's flag, it now hangs in the National Museum of American History, which is part of the Smithsonian Institution, in Washington, D.C.

Peace Seems Unlikely

In the nation's charred capital, President Madison's government floundered helplessly, not knowing where the British would strike next. The president himself, a visitor wrote, looked "miserably shattered and woebegone. In short, he looks broken-hearted."[10] It was fully expected that the British would renew their invasion by way of Lake Champlain, and it was no secret that they also planned to attack somewhere near New Orleans, Louisiana. Daniel Webster,

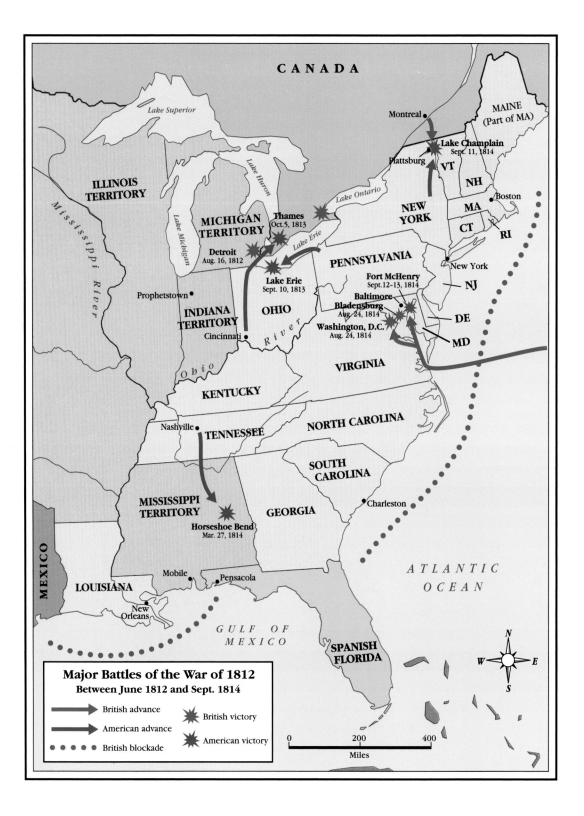

CANADA

Lake Superior

ILLINOIS
TERRITORY

Lake Huron

Mississippi River

MICHIGAN
TERRITORY

Thames
Oct. 5, 1813

Lake Erie

Detroit
Aug. 16, 1812

Lake Erie
Sept. 10, 1813

Prophetstown •

INDIANA
TERRITORY

OHIO

Ohio River

Cincinnati •

KENTUCKY

Nashville •

TENNESSEE

Lake Ontario

Montreal •

Lake Champlain
Sept. 11, 1814

Plattsburg •

MAINE
(Part of MA)

VT

NH

• Boston

NEW
YORK

MA

CT

RI

PENNSYLVANIA

• New York

Fort McHenry
Sept.12-13, 1814

NJ

Baltimore
Bladensburg
Aug. 24, 1814

Washington, D.C.
Aug. 24, 1814

DE

MD

VIRGINIA

NORTH CAROLINA

SOUTH
CAROLINA

• Charleston

MISSISSIPPI
TERRITORY

Horseshoe Bend
Mar. 27, 1814

GEORGIA

MEXICO

LOUISIANA

New
Orleans •

Mobile •

Pensacola •

*GULF OF
MEXICO*

SPANISH
FLORIDA

*ATLANTIC
OCEAN*

N
W   E
S

Major Battles of the War of 1812
Between June 1812 and Sept. 1814

→ British advance
➡ American advance
•••• British blockade

✦ British victory
✸ American victory

0   200   400
Miles

< 21 >

who was then a young congressman, predicted, "If Peace does not come this winter, the Government will die of its own weakness."[11]

Hopes for peace, however, were as dim as the nation's prospects for winning the war. A team of negotiators had been meeting with British delegates in Ghent, Belgium, since August 1814, but the British negotiators were making unreasonable demands. They wanted a peace treaty that would create a Native American buffer state between Canada and the United States, to be located south of the Great Lakes. They also wanted part of Maine annexed to Canada. Although the Americans were not in a good position to bargain, they would not even consider such harsh terms.

On the home front, opposition to the war had become so fierce that it threatened to break up the United States. Anti-war Federalists in New England called for a convention to meet at Hartford in December 1814. Delegates to this Hartford Convention were willing to consider separating New England from the rest of the states.

President Madison was in desperate need of some hopeful sign. The successful defense of Fort McHenry and the naval victory on Lake Champlain seemed to be only temporary reprieves from further British actions. The president had to find some way to protect New Orleans from the expected invasion. The needs of the president, and the nation, were to be met by a new military leader—Andrew Jackson, of Tennessee.

James Madison

PART TWO

NEW ORLEANS:
"ONE OF THE MOST BRILLIANT VICTORIES"

In the autumn of 1814, a British fleet gathered off Jamaica, in the Caribbean, to prepare for the largest campaign of the war—the capture of New Orleans. A decisive victory there, Admiral Cochrane predicted, "would drive the Americans entirely out of Louisiana and the Floridas," and force them to accept Britain's terms for peace.[1]

The American government knew the British were planning an invasion somewhere in the Gulf of Mexico. Since New Orleans was a vital seaport for all the American states and territories west of the Appalachian Mountains, it seemed the natural target. In September, President Madison ordered the nation's newest major general, Andrew Jackson, to prepare for a British attack somewhere in the vicinity of New Orleans.

The British knew almost nothing about Jackson. Neither did most Americans. While the two nations had been battling each other in the North, Jackson had been waging a very different war in the South against the Creeks, the most powerful of the Indian nations.

Jackson and the "Red Sticks"

Beginning in 1812, and picking up momentum in 1813, hundreds of young Creek warriors were stirred to action by visits from the Shawnee chief Tecumseh. They launched a series of raids against settlements in Georgia and the Mississippi Territory (which included present-day Alabama). The warriors, known as the "Red Sticks" because of their red war clubs, spread terror throughout the southwestern frontier. Settlers abandoned their farms and gathered together in quickly assembled forts.

< 23 >

The massacre at Fort Mims was one of the bloodiest raids made by the Indians known as the Red Sticks.

On August 30, 1813, the Red Sticks attacked one of these, Fort Mims, located 40 miles north of Mobile. Of the nearly 600 settlers in the fort, only 17 escaped. The Creek carried 250 scalps out of the fort on poles.

Andrew Jackson, a tough frontier lawyer, soldier, and former senator from Tennessee, responded to this attack by leading a force of 2,500 of his state's militia into Creek territory. Although weak from a gunshot wound suffered in a street brawl three weeks earlier, Jackson pushed his men hard, fighting a series of inconclusive battles between November 1813 and January 1814.

In March 1814, Jackson's troops were reinforced by a U.S. Army regiment and a Tennessee cavalry unit (soldiers on horseback), led by

Major John Coffee. The combined force attacked the main Creek army at a place called Horseshoe Bend, on the Tallapoosa River. In the battle of Horseshoe Bend on March 27, the U.S. forces over-whelmed the 1,200 Red Sticks, killing 600 and taking 350 prisoner. Even Jackson, a veteran soldier, felt that "the carnage was dreadful."[2]

The battle of Horseshoe Bend destroyed the Creek nation as a fighting force. In August 1814, Jackson dictated his harsh terms for peace, forcing the Creek chiefs to give over rights to 23 million acres of land to the U.S. government.

The U.S. victory at Horseshoe Bend temporarily restored peace to the frontier, and it also affected the contest for New Orleans. First, the battle deprived the British of a valuable potential ally. They had assumed that several thousand Creek would join their invasion force as soon as it landed. Second, as a result of Jackson's leadership in the Creek War, President Madison made Jackson a major general in the U.S. Army.

Preparations for Battle

General Jackson had his own ideas about preparing for the British invasion. He thought the attack was most likely to come at Mobile, not New Orleans, so he rushed there to strengthen Fort Bowyer, which protected the town of 3,000 to 4,000 people. Satisfied that the fort was so strong that "ten thousand men cannot take it," he left.[3] Jackson was right. On September 12, 1814, when a small British naval and land force tried to capture the fort, they caused little damage, but lost one ship and nearly 100 men.

Jackson next led a force of 3,000 to Pensacola in Spanish Florida. This was a totally unauthorized invasion of neutral Spain's possession, but he had learned that a British unit had landed at Pensacola to enlist the aid of the Creek and other tribes. When the

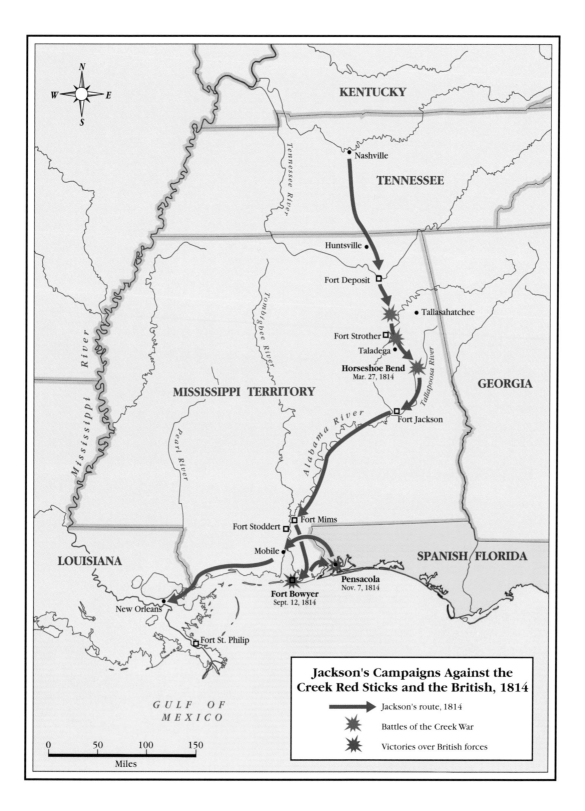

KENTUCKY

TENNESSEE

• Nashville

Huntsville •

Tennessee River

Fort Deposit □

× • Tallasahatchee

Fort Strother □ ×

Taladega •

Horseshoe Bend
Mar. 27, 1814

Tallapoosa River

GEORGIA

MISSISSIPPI TERRITORY

Tombigbee River

Alabama River

Fort Jackson □

Mississippi River

Pearl River

□ Fort Mims

Fort Stoddert □

Mobile •

SPANISH FLORIDA

LOUISIANA

□ Pensacola
Fort Bowyer Nov. 7, 1814
Sept. 12, 1814

New Orleans

□ Fort St. Philip

GULF OF MEXICO

| 0 | 50 | 100 | 150 |

Miles

Jackson's Campaigns Against the Creek Red Sticks and the British, 1814

➤ Jackson's route, 1814

✷ Battles of the Creek War

✷ Victories over British forces

small British force saw Jackson's troops approaching, the British blew up the town's decaying fort and fled. Any hope the British had of Indian support was shattered when the Indians saw how quickly the British fled from Pensacola.

Finally Jackson was ready to head for New Orleans. On the way, he sent urgent messages to the governors of Tennessee, Kentucky, and the Mississippi Territory, asking for militia troops. He arrived in New Orleans on December 1, 1814, and found that most of the city's people were gripped by a combination of fear and an unwillingness to act. Only a handful of men had responded to the governor's call for militia.

New Orleans had become part

Since its earliest days, the city of New Orleans has been home to people from a wide variety of cultural traditions.

of the United States in 1803 under the terms of the Louisiana Purchase. The large tract of land that the United States acquired from France more than doubled the size of the American nation. Before the French possessed it, Louisiana was occupied by the Spanish government. As a result, New Orleans, a city of 10,000, was populated by a rich mixture of diverse ethnic groups. In addition to French, Spanish, and American settlers, New Orleans was home to escaped slaves from southern plantations, black refugees from battles of the Napoleonic Wars in the Caribbean islands, Cajuns (French Canadians who were forced from their homes by the British in the eighteenth

Througout his life, Andrew Jackson displayed extraordinary courage and determination. By the age of 14, he had lost his family in the bitter warfare of the American Revolution, which he fought in. Jackson had very little formal schooling. Living in North Carolina, he taught himself the law and was admitted to practice in 1787, at the age of 20. He let no obstacle stand in the way of his drive for success in everything he tried.

Jackson moved to the frontier town of Nashville and served briefly (from 1796 to 1798) in Congress for the new state of Tennessee. He also found time to speculate in land, buying and selling property, and he established a plantation he called the Hermitage.

Andrew Jackson

In 1804, Jackson retired from public life but served as a major general of the state's militia. Unlike other militia officers who usually treated their positions as honorary ones, Jackson enthusiastically studied military history and tactics. At the start of the War of 1812, he offered to raise a militia force of 2,500, but the government chose to ignore him, probably because he had not supported James Madison in the 1808 presidential election.

During the Creek War, Jackson seemed single-minded in his

century), and German immigrants. While this blending of peoples and cultures gave New Orleans much of its charm and vitality, it seemed to be impossible for these ethnic groups to unite against a common danger. Many of the people seemed lulled by the hope that other states would save them. Louisiana had been admitted as a state just a few weeks before the War of 1812 was declared.

determination to win. At one point, some of his militia troops insisted they were going home because their enlistments were up. Jackson and two other officers threatened them with a pair of cannons, refusing to let them leave.

Jackson also displayed a kinder side during that war. In December 1813, when he was ordered to disband his force and return to Tennessee, he would not leave his men. He used $3,000 of his own money to buy supplies and wagons for the sick. He even gave his horse to a militiaman too ill to make the journey on foot, and Jackson walked the 800-mile-long journey with his men. "He's as tough as hickory," one of the men said.[4] The label stuck, and for the rest of his life Jackson was known as "Old Hickory."

As a national hero after the battle of New Orleans, Jackson seemed to embody the spirit of frontier equality and democracy. People simply ignored the fact that he was a wealthy man who owned both a plantation and slaves. He was swept into the presidency in 1828 on the wave of democratic reforms that would later be labeled "Jacksonian democracy."

Jackson was a man of contradictions. He believed that he treated Native Americans fairly, even though he was the architect of the Indian Removal policy that forced all of the eastern tribes to move west of the Mississippi. Hailed as a democrat, he remained a slave owner. And even though he did own slaves, Jackson's last words spoke of equality: "I hope to see you all in Heaven, both white and black."[5]

Jackson Inspires the People of New Orleans

The apathy quickly disappeared when Jackson arrived. Although he was now suffering from dysentery, he spent his first few days in New Orleans on horseback, studying the terrain and issuing a seemingly endless stream of orders. The power of his personality had a definite effect. Men now flocked to sign up for the militia, and

Andrew Jackson inspired the citizens of New Orleans to defend themselves against the British.

Jackson allowed the formation of a battalion of "free men of color." The women of New Orleans were inspired to take action, too; they hastily transformed 1,200 blankets into coats, vests, and pants for the troops.

Obstacles to Overcome

The enthusiasm of the people was encouraging, but Jackson knew that the forces at his disposal were far from adequate. When he reviewed the troops, he found many without uniforms or weapons. Some companies, however, were clearly well disciplined and equipped, including one African-Creole unit that had been formed several years earlier. There were also 500 regulars from the army's Forty-Fourth Regiment and a small navy detachment under Commodore Daniel T. Patterson.

All together, the defense force numbered less than 1,500 men. Jackson could only hope that the help he had sent for would arrive before the British did. John Coffee was on the way with his 1,200-man Tennessee cavalry and another 2,000-man Tennessee force under militia Brigadier General William Carroll was making the 1,300-mile journey down the Mississippi River. A large unit of Kentucky militia was also reported to be on the way.

Shortage of manpower was not the Americans' only problem. The troops were woefully short of weapons and ammunition. In addition, the complex terrain of the Mississippi Delta—the fan-shaped

< 31 >

area where the river entered the sea—made it impossible to tell what direction the British would be coming from. New Orleans was located nearly 100 miles north of the mouth of the Mississippi, and the entire region was honeycombed with rivers, swamps, canals, creeks, and bayous (sluggish streams that fed into the Mississippi and the Gulf of Mexico). There were also two lakes in the area—Lake Pontchartrain and Lake Borgne—navigable only by shallow-water boats.

It was clear to Jackson that his best chance of saving the city was to concentrate his troops in one place for a decisive battle, but only if *he* could choose the location for that battle. This meant Jackson had to have enough advance notice of the British approach to be able to lure them onto the ground he chose. He established an early-warning system by sending small detachments to watch over the major approaches to the city.

As part of this warning system, Commodore Patterson sent six gunboats (small sailing vessels, each armed with four guns) onto Lake Borgne, a small body of water that opened onto the Gulf. On December 11, the commander of the gunboats sent word to New Orleans that an enormous British fleet was in sight.

The British Approach

The British invasion fleet, made up of 50 ships, carried 20,000 soldiers, sailors, and marines—the largest force the British had ever sent against America. The fleet was commanded by Admiral Cochrane, and the 8,000-man invasion force would be led by Major General Sir Edward Pakenham, although he would not arrive for another two weeks.

Powerful as this armada was, it faced some serious problems. Cochrane and the army's temporary commander, Major General John

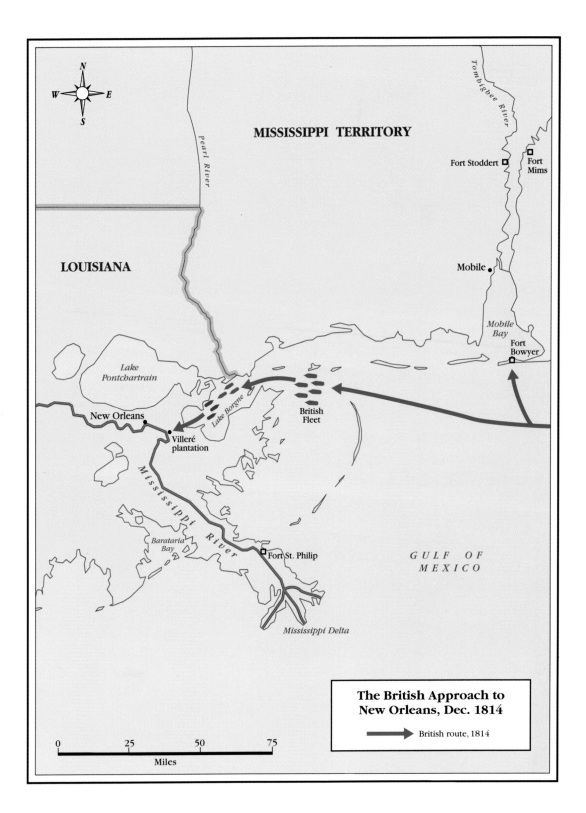

N
W   E
S

MISSISSIPPI TERRITORY

Tombigbee River

Fort Stoddert ◻   ◻ Fort Mims

LOUISIANA

Pearl River

Mobile •

Mobile Bay

◻ Fort Bowyer

Lake Pontchartrain

New Orleans •

Lake Borgne

British Fleet

Villeré plantation

Mississippi River

Barataria Bay

◻ Fort St. Philip

GULF OF MEXICO

Mississippi Delta

The British Approach to New Orleans, Dec. 1814

→ British route, 1814

0   25   50   75

Miles

< 33 >

Keane, decided that the best approach to New Orleans was through Lake Borgne. But the entrance to the lake was too shallow for the ships. This meant that the entire invasion force would have to be transferred to shallow-water launches or barges and rowed onto the lake. Throughout the campaign, the British ships, including the five British men-of-war—each with at least 70 guns (cannons)—would remain at anchor some 80 miles from New Orleans.

By December 14, the British had 45 vessels on Lake Borgne, and they quickly forced the 6 American gunboats into surrender. When this news reached New Orleans, the people were close to panic, and there was talk of surrendering the city. Jackson responded by issuing a proclamation stating, "It is true the enemy is on our coast and threatens an invasion of our territory, but it is equally true, with union, energy, and the approbation of Heaven, we will beat him at every point."[6] Jackson also declared martial law—which temporarily puts the civil government on hold and gives all power to the military—and declared that any able-bodied man who did not appear with a firearm would be considered a friend of the British.

By December 20, the American defense force was strengthened by the arrival of the two Tennessee militia units under John Coffee,

Low-water barges were used to transport British soldiers and artillery from their ships to Lake Borgne.

< 34 >

now a militia general, and General Carroll. Coffee's men were quickly labeled "the Dirty Shirts" because, as one observer wrote, they were "wearing woolen hunting-shirts of dark or dingy color... with slouching wool hats, some composed of skins of raccoons and foxes...[and] with belts of untanned deer-skin, in which were stuck hunting-knives and tomahawks."[7] While the people may have wondered about these men, Jackson knew, from his experience with them at the battle of Horseshoe Bend, that they were among the best fighters in the country.

Jean Lafitte Offers Help

The Americans received help from an unexpected source when Jean Lafitte, a notorious pirate and smuggler, offered his services and those of his men. Lafitte and his brothers held a strong position on a bay called Barataria in the Gulf of Mexico. From there, they smuggled goods and raided Spanish merchant ships. They often sold their goods at auctions in New Orleans.

Both pirates and smugglers, Jean Lafitte (right) and his men had great wealth and large supplies of ammunition.

Jackson accepted Lafitte's offer. He was desperate for men, and he knew the "Baratarians" were expert fighters with cannons. Lafitte ordered that the pirates' ample supply of ammunition be transferred to the Americans. These new allies were to be of critical importance in the coming battle.

While Jackson was organizing his defensive forces, British General Keane was moving an advance force up one

Several times each year during the early 1800s, the wealthier citizens of New Orleans traveled south of the city to a place called "the Temple," an ancient Indian shell mound. There, the well-dressed French and Americans mingled with a rough band of smugglers and pirates. Their leader was a tall, handsome, well-mannered Frenchman named Jean Lafitte.

The people came to the Temple for Lafitte's fabulous auctions. They could buy the finest jewels, silver, wines, mahogany, and silks—all free of customs duties (taxes). Orders for Lafitte's goods came from as far away as New York and Philadelphia.

By 1815, Jean Lafitte and his two brothers had been operating their illegal trade for a dozen years. From their well-fortified base at Barataria Bay, near the mouth of the Mississippi, they controlled more than two dozen armed ships and a force of more than 3,000 men. They amassed wealth and power by smuggling goods for traders around the world who didn't want to pay customs taxes, and by seizing Spanish ships on the Gulf of Mexico. In the process, many of the Baratarians became experts with cannons of every size and description.

Because the Lafittes were so popular in New Orleans, it was hard for Louisiana Governor William Claiborne to take action against them. While the governor might have tolerated the customs-free auctions, he was opposed to the Baratarians' illegal smuggling of slaves. Claiborne finally succeeded in sending an army and naval force against the Baratarians. Lafitte had enough advance notice to remove most of his men, cannons, and ammunition. But the Americans did seize several of his ships, a fortune in treasure, and Jean's two brothers. The desire to gain a pardon for himself and his men was behind Lafitte's offer to help Jackson in the defense of New Orleans.

After the Baratarians displayed their skill and courage in the battle, President Madison granted a full pardon to Jean Lafitte and his followers. The pardon, however, did not change Lafitte's ways. He established a new base at what is now Galveston, Texas, and continued his career as smuggler and pirate.

In 1821, the U.S. government took action against the pirate once again. Just as before, Lafitte had advance notice. He sailed away on his favorite ship, *Pride*, and his exploits thereafter are clouded by mystery and legend. Most historians believe he moved to the coast of Mexico and died there.

< 36 >

of the bayous. These soldiers, toughened in the war against Napoleon, struggled heroically over the swampy terrain, exposed to torrential rains during the day and freezing cold at night. In the two black West Indies regiments, an estimated 200 men, unused to the frigid nights, died of exposure or pneumonia.

On December 22, the British stormed a plantation owned by the Villeré family and made this their base for the assault on New Orleans. Gustav Villeré managed to leap out a window, borrow a neighbor's horse, and gallop to New Orleans with the news that the advance British force was now less than eight miles from the city.

First Clashes

Most military commanders would have responded to Villeré's news by moving into defensive positions. Jackson did just the opposite. "By the Eternal!" he thundered, "they shall not sleep on our soil! Gentlemen, the British are below. We must fight them tonight."[8]

As darkness fell, Jackson led a force of 2,100 men toward the Villeré plantation, while Commodore Patterson floated his ship *Carolina* downstream, close to the plantation. The 1,700 British, exhausted and cold, were just finishing their evening meal when shells from the *Carolina* began crashing into their camp. At the same time, the American land troops opened fire, and Coffee's men moved in.

The British scrambled for their weapons and for the cover of a levee—a bank built up near a river to prevent flooding. A British officer described the scene:

All order, all discipline were lost. Each officer, as he succeeded in collecting twenty or thirty men about him, plunged into the midst of the enemy's ranks, where it was fought hand to hand, bayonet to bayonet, and sabre to sabre.[9]

MAJOR GENERAL SIR EDWARD PAKENHAM: "NOT THE GREATEST GENIUS"

Major General Sir Edward Pakenham, the leader of the British expedition against New Orleans, had learned battle strategy from his brother-in-law the Duke of Wellington. (Wellington was perhaps the greatest general in British history. He was also married to Kitty Pakenham, Sir Edward's sister.) Wellington wrote of Pakenham, "[He] may not be the greatest genius but…he is one of the best we have."[10] That seems a fair assessment of the general. With a touch of Wellington's genius he might have avoided the disastrous losses suffered by the British at New Orleans.

As the younger son of British nobility, Ned Pakenham did not inherit the money or the seat in Parliament that eldest sons were entitled to. He chose a military career, entering the army when he was 16 years old. He gradually worked his way up through the ranks and spent most of his career fighting against France in the Napoleonic Wars, which kept the British busy from 1793 until the defeat of Napoleon in 1815. In 1812, at the age of 34, he was promoted to the rank of major general. Two years later, in recognition of his strong service under Wellington, he was given command of the New Orleans expedition.

Pakenham's decisions during that campaign played right into Andrew Jackson's hands. Military historians say that if Pakenham had ordered an attack as soon as he arrived at the Villeré plantation, the Americans would not have been prepared. Instead, he delayed to bring artillery from the fleet, giving the defenders time to dig in behind the Rodriguez Canal. Then, when the British artillery failed even to dent the American defenses, he should have known that a frontal assault could not succeed.

One reason Pakenham ordered the attack was his confidence that inexperienced American militiamen would turn and run in the face of a disciplined charge by his seasoned veterans. He has been criticized for that assumption ever since. Hugh Brogan, a modern British historian, describes Pakenham's decision with a touch of sarcasm:

> He devised a magnificent plan of attack that had the single disadvantage of being unworkable; then he hurled his devoted troops against Jackson's well-prepared trenches. All the Americans had to do was shoot down the assailants as they came…. Then the British crawled off to the safety of their ships, and the Americans rejoiced.[11]

< 38 >

The battle turned into a standoff. Before dawn, Jackson learned that British reinforcements were approaching, and he ordered his men to withdraw. The startled British troops had responded well, but 276 of them were killed or wounded, twice as many casualties as the Americans. The British also discovered that they were facing a far more determined enemy than they had expected.

The next day, December 24, 1814, General Pakenham arrived to take command from Keane. In spite of the American attack, Pakenham was confident that his experienced troops would easily overwhelm the American defenses. He decided to pause only long enough for the rest of the army to move up to the Villeré plantation, bringing cannons and ammunition with them.

No one on either side could know that, on that same evening, the American and British peace negotiators in Ghent, Belgium, had signed a treaty ending the war. For the men laboring to prepare for battle at New Orleans, news of peace would arrive too late.

While Pakenham readied his attack on New Orleans, Jackson established his defensive line on a narrow strip of land behind the Rodriguez Canal. This canal, which had once been used to supply river water for a mill, was now a dry, grass-covered ditch 12 feet wide and varying in depth from 4 to 8 feet. The moat-like ditch stretched from the river levee 2,700 feet inland, where it ended in a dense, thickly wooded swamp.

Behind the canal, the Americans worked furiously to build a rampart, or barricade, of fallen logs with earth packed between. To provide level, solid platforms for their cannons, they used cotton bales covered with more earth. At the same time, the *Carolina* and a smaller ship, the *Louisiana*, continued to bombard the British camp.

Hampered by the steady cannonade from the two ships, Pakenham's men also had trouble making emplacements—solid, level positions with protection for the gun crews and their 30 cannons.

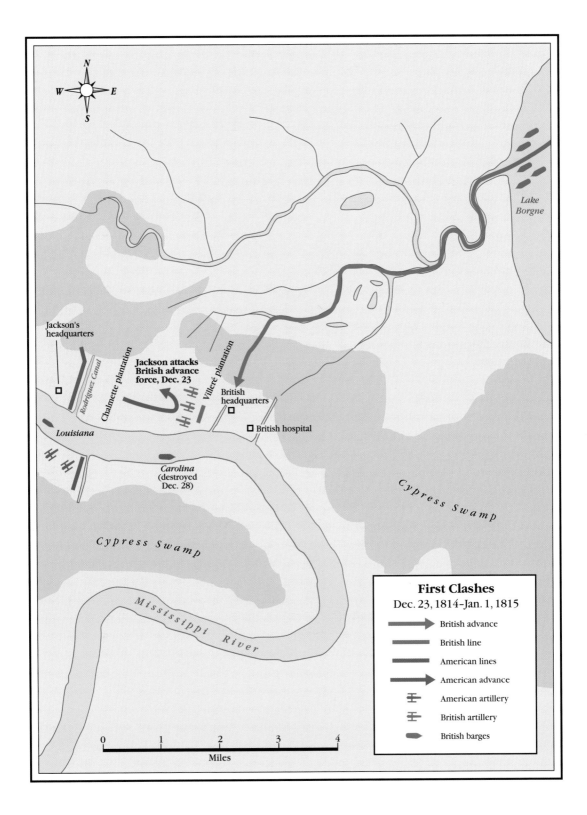

N
W   E
S

Lake
Borgne

Jackson's
headquarters

Rodriguez Canal

Chalmette plantation

**Jackson attacks
British advance
force, Dec. 23**

Villeré plantation

British
headquarters

British hospital

Louisiana

Carolina
(destroyed
Dec. 28)

C y p r e s s   S w a m p

C y p r e s s   S w a m p

M i s s i s s i p p i   R i v e r

First Clashes
Dec. 23, 1814–Jan. 1, 1815

British advance

British line

American lines

American advance

American artillery

British artillery

British barges

0   1   2   3   4

Miles

< 40 >

The cannons had been hauled nearly 80 miles from the fleet. When the British dug holes, water rapidly seeped in, so they were forced to build above ground and use sugar barrels packed with earth to give the artillery crews a little protection.

On December 28, the British gunners shot at the *Carolina* and *Louisiana* with heated cannonballs, called "hot shot." These cannonballs were heated over an open flame until red-hot and would set whatever they hit on fire. (Cold cannonballs would only start a fire if they hit something explosive.) The British were able to set the *Carolina* ablaze, but the *Louisiana* managed to get upstream out of cannon range. Pakenham's troops advanced toward the American lines, but were quickly ordered back because of the Americans' heavy cannon fire.

By the end of the month, Pakenham felt ready to move forward. On December 31, a naval officer stationed with the general sent a confident note to Admiral Cochrane: "The General proposes to move tomorrow at daylight.... I think he will be in possession of New Orleans tomorrow night—he appears determined on a bold push."[12]

On January 1, 1815, the British cannons opened fire. On the British left, General Keane advanced with one brigade, and Major General Samuel Gibbs moved on the right with another. If the artillery weakened the American line, these two forces would attack. Instead, the British found themselves hopelessly pinned down by the American cannons, a couple of them manned by Lafitte's skillful Baratarians. To create a deadly crossfire, Commodore Patterson used the *Louisiana*'s guns on one side and two cannons that he had placed on the far shore of the Mississippi on the other. British Lieutenant George Gleig described the impact of the American artillery:

Scarce a ball passed over or fell short of its mark, but all striking full into the midst of our ranks, occasioned terrible havoc. The

< 41 >

shrieks of the wounded…the crash of firelocks [muskets]*, and the fall of such that were killed, caused…confusion; and what added to the panic was that from the houses beside which we stood bright flames suddenly burst out…. Two large chateaux and their out-buildings almost scorched us with the flames, and blinded us with the smoke which they emitted.*[13]

After three hours of this artillery duel, the British were nearly out of ammunition and Pakenham ordered a withdrawal back to the Villeré plantation. The British army's failure to silence the American artillery was a serious blow to the British hopes of winning the battle. As Gleig noted in his journal, "We retired…not only baffled and disappointed, but in some degree disheartened. All our plans had as yet proved abortive."[14]

Pakenham decided to wait for the arrival of one more brigade of reinforcements before attacking again. The delay gave the Americans time to finish their defenses and to build two reserve lines north of the city. The reserve lines were barricades where the Americans could set up their defenses if they had to retreat in the face of a successful attack. During this lull, the American General John Thomas arrived in New Orleans with 2,300 Kentucky militiamen, but Jackson was horrified to find that two-thirds of them had no weapons. Still, they added manpower, and Jackson sent part of this force to the far bank of the river to strengthen the artillery position there. The Americans were ready for the main British assault.

January 8, 1815: The Final Battle

For the major assault on the American lines, Pakenham added something new to his strategy. He planned to send 1,100 men under Colonel William Thornton across the Mississippi to attack the

< 42 >

American artillery position on the riverbank. Once captured, those two guns could then be turned on the American defensive line at the Rodriguez Canal.

Once again, however, the terrain worked against the British. They had to cut a canal across the levee to drag boats through for the crossing. As dawn approached on January 8, only a handful of Thornton's men had made it across the river.

Pakenham faced a difficult decision. His main force was poised to attack. Did he dare order them to withdraw one more time? Or should he proceed, even if Thornton's unit failed to silence the American battery? The general's aide, Sir Harry Smith, urged him to withdraw.

Pakenham answered, "I have twice deferred the attack. We are strong in numbers.... If Thornton fails, it will cost more men, but the assault must be made."[15] In terms of strategy, morale, and British pride, the commander thought that it was now too late to withdraw. As the first streaks of morning light appeared on the horizon, he ordered the attack.

The British advanced once more with Keane's brigade on the left. The two fresh regiments of reinforcements, under General John Lambert, were briefly held in reserve in the center—except for a small assault force led by Colonel Robert Dale—but followed the rest of the troops shortly after the advance.

Pakenham arranged for Gibbs's men to lead the major attack on the right (against the American left). During the January 1 artillery duel, he had noticed through his telescope that the American left was held by men in hunting shirts. Pakenham thought the shirts marked them as militiamen who were likely to run away in the face of a disciplined charge. He did not know that those men were Coffee's Dirty Shirts, and that they were armed with rifles that were far more accurate than the British muskets.

< 43 >

Jackson's rag-tag army, now numbering about 5,000, was arrayed behind the Rodriguez Canal. Regular soldiers anchored the right of the American line. The only other regulars, the Forty-Fourth Regiment, held the center. Between them were the New Orleans militia, the two battalions of "free colored," dozens of the Baratarian pirates at the cannons, and a unit of 68 New Orleans lawyers and merchants. The Tennesseans, under Coffee and Carroll, held the left, closest to the cypress swamp.

British General Gibbs had chosen an experienced regiment, the Forty-Fourth (not to be confused with the American Forty-Fourth Regiment), to lead the assault on Coffee's position. The regiment's commander, Lieutenant Colonel Thomas Mullens, predicted the failure of the mission, grumbling to his officers, "The 44th will have the forlorn hope.... I think they will catch it."[16]

From behind their defenses at the Rodriguez Canal, the Americans held off the British assault.

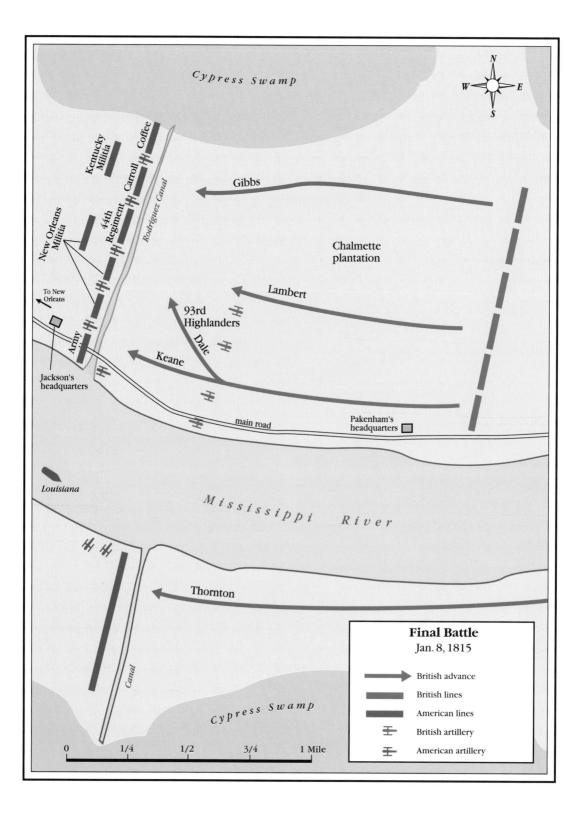

Cypress Swamp

N
W · E
S

Kentucky Militia

Gibbs

Coffee
Carroll
44th Regiment

New Orleans Militia

Rodriguez Canal

Chalmette plantation

To New Orleans

Lambert

93rd Highlanders

Dale

Army

Keane

Jackson's headquarters

main road

Pakenham's headquarters

Louisiana

M i s s i s s i p p i   R i v e r

Thornton

Canal

Cypress Swamp

| 0 | 1/4 | 1/2 | 3/4 | 1 Mile |

Final Battle
Jan. 8, 1815

British advance

British lines

American lines

British artillery

American artillery

< 45 >

At 3:30 A.M., a signal rocket flared into the predawn gloom, and the British advance began. But, incredibly, Mullens had misunderstood his orders and failed to bring along 16 scaling ladders and 300 fascines—bundles of sticks used in scaling an entrenched position. When he realized his mistake, he frantically sent men back for this vitally important equipment, but it was too late. The attack was already underway.

The cannons on both sides thundered, and the British, cheering wildly, rushed forward in columns 60 men wide and 8 deep. Added to the roar of the cannons was the crack of rifles and muskets, the steady drumbeat of the British regimental drummers, and the bagpipes of the Scottish Ninety-Third Highlanders. Above the din, the Americans could hear Jackson shouting encouragement: "Give it to them, boys! Let's finish this business today!"[17]

The advance guard of Gibbs's brigade leaped into the canal and tried to climb the American rampart in a bayonet charge. But they had no scaling ladders or fascines. The men behind them stopped and began shooting at the American defenses, exposing themselves to the rifle fire of the Tennesseans. "Some of our men," one Tennessean recalled, "discharged their weapons without raising their heads above the rampart. The redcoats were so tightly packed, it would have been hard to miss."[18]

The men of the British Forty-Fourth hesitated, then turned and ran. Gibbs spurred his horse forward, trying to rally the men, and shouted for Mullens: "Colonel Mullens, if I live to see tomorrow you shall be hanged from one of these trees!"[19] Seconds later, four bullets ripped into his body and he toppled to the ground.

General Pakenham saw that Gibbs's brigade was in trouble and ordered Keane to use part of his force to help. This meant that Keane's men would have to move all the way across the battlefield, and would be completely exposed to the American artillery and

< 46 >

rifles. But Keane obeyed, and the Ninety-Third Highlanders, in their distinctive tartan plaid, broke into a run as the bagpipes played the regimental charge. It was a brave and foolish maneuver. As one of the survivors of the Ninety-Third wrote,

> *The enemy...no sooner got us within 150 yards of their works than a most destructive and murderous fire was opened on our Column of round, grape* [clusters of iron pellets shot from cannons], *musketry, rifle, and buckshot along the whole course and length of our line in front; as well as on our left flank.*[20]

One of the American regulars recalled, "Foolheardy as they were, we had to admire their bravery, for they ran right into the teeth of our guns which tore great holes in their ranks."[21]

In a frantic effort to save the assault, Pakenham came forward, waving his hat and shouting, "Remember, you are British soldiers! This is the road to take!"[22]

Major General Sir Edward Pakenham urges his troops onward.

< 47 >

A volley of gunfire shattered the general's knee and killed his horse. An aide helped him up and onto another horse, but he was instantly struck three more times and died on the field. Moments later, Keane also went down, seriously wounded. Dale, rushing to help, was killed as well. Of the 950 Highlanders who had set out to help Gibbs, only 125 stumbled back to the British lines.

With all of the assault officers dead or wounded, General Lambert was now in command. His two reserve regiments, which had followed close behind the attacking unit, were already suffering heavy casualties. Sickened by the sight of the field covered with dead or dying British, Lambert ordered a withdrawal. On the far side of the river, Thornton's men had finally taken control of the American artillery position, but that one success came too late to save the British, and Thornton's men also withdrew.

The battle of New Orleans was over only hours after it began, and the men on both sides were stunned by how overwhelming the American victory was. Jackson's troops had suffered only 71 casualties, including 13 dead. Of the nearly 8,000 men in the British attack, more than 500 had been killed, an estimated 2,000 wounded, and 484 taken prisoner. Among the British casualties were 3 generals, 11 colonels, and 75 officers of lesser rank.

A truce was declared to care for the wounded, bury the dead, and arrange for the exchange of prisoners. (In order to avoid having to set up camps to take care of enemies captured during battle, prisoners were often exchanged as quickly as possible during the War of 1812.) As the British began their slow withdrawal to their fleet, many of the Americans wanted to go after them, confident they could carry their triumph even further. But Jackson knew better than to let his men emerge from the protection of their ramparts and artillery to fight experienced British soldiers in the open. The British attempt to capture New Orleans was finished.

< 48 >

The Americans stayed in battle-ready position for two more weeks. Then most of the militia disbanded, and the U.S. Army stayed on for a few weeks. On March 6, 1815, nearly two months after the battle, official word of the peace treaty arranged in Ghent finally reached New Orleans.

The Aftermath

Because news traveled so slowly in the early 1800s, word of the resounding American victory at New Orleans did not reach Washington, D.C., until late on February 4. The next day church bells rang, the cannons of Baltimore's Fort McHenry boomed a salute, and people everywhere celebrated in the streets.

News of the peace treaty ending the war arrived in the nation's capital six days later, touching off another round of joyous celebration. (This length of time for news to cross the Atlantic was not unusual. News of the Treaty of Paris, which ended the Revolutionary War, took four months to reach Philadelphia from Paris.) An unpopular war that had carried the nation to the brink of disaster was ending on a triumphant note. It did not matter that the victory at New Orleans had been won 15 days after the treaty was signed. General Jackson had told his men that their heroic stand would be remembered "as one of the most brilliant victories in the annals of the war."[23] To the American people, the battle of New Orleans meant even more than that. It gave them the distinct feeling they had won the war.

The battle, of course, had no bearing on the peace treaty, known as the Treaty of Ghent. By the terms of the treaty, neither side gained or lost anything. All boundaries were restored to their 1812 locations. Nothing was said about free trade or the rights of sailors. And yet, in a very real sense, Americans could say they had won "a second

< 49 >

War for Independence" because they had finally won the grudging respect of Europe, especially Great Britain. James Bayard, a leading Federalist, explained the nation's new status in a letter to his son:

> *The war raised our reputation in Europe, and it excites astonishment that we should have been able...to have fought Great Britain single handed.... I think it will be a long time before we are disturbed again by any of the powers of Europe.*[24]

Bayard was right. American and British troops would not meet again for 100 years, and then it would be as allies on the battlefields of World War I (1914–1918). Future disputes over boundaries and other matters were settled by conferences, as provided for in the Treaty of Ghent.

Not only did the war and its final battle improve the nation's standing in the world; they also gave Americans a new sense of national pride and unity. Instead of splintering into sections, the nation emerged more united than ever before.

The high points of the War of 1812—the naval battles of Lake Erie and Lake Champlain, the exploits of warships like the *Constitution*, the heroic defense of Fort McHenry and the writing of the "Star-Spangled Banner," and perhaps greatest of all, the battle of New Orleans—were all building blocks in establishing a new sense of patriotism. As a French diplomat put it, "Finally, the war has given the Americans what they so essentially lacked—a national character founded on a glory common to all."[25]

The battle of New Orleans had one other significant result—the emergence of Andrew Jackson as the nation's greatest hero since George Washington. Thirteen years later, he became the seventh president of the United States, and the first from the region west of the Appalachian Mountains.

HISTORY REMEMBERED

America's national battlefield parks provide us with vivid explorations into some of the most dramatic moments in our nation's history. They preserve the scenes of great triumphs and tragedies—episodes of extraordinary heroism and courage, intermingled with examples of costly blunders and fatal errors of judgment.

The wonder of America's battlefield parks and monuments is their ability to carry visitors back in time, enabling those visitors to see and feel the ebb and flow of conflicts that have shaped our history and preserved and strengthened our democracy. Each site also serves as a memorial to the men—and some women—who fought and died for their vision of America.

In the early 1990s, federal budget cutbacks led to a crisis in many of the parks and monuments. Hours of operation were reduced, funds were cut back for salaries and the development of displays, and the very existence of several key sites was threatened. The American people, however, made it clear that the preservation of these places is a treasured part of their national heritage. In response to the appeals of many voters and organizations, budgets have been restored and the personnel at many sites are making important renovations. Facilities for handicapped visitors have been improved, for example, and many displays now make use of the latest in audiovisual and computer technology.

Jean Lafitte National Historical Park and Preserve, Chalmette Unit

The park is located about six miles east of New Orleans, on what was known as the Chalmette Plantation, the plantation that was closest to the Rodriguez Canal defenses. At the Visitors Center, a 28-minute film

< 51 >

The reconstructed American defenses along the Rodriguez Canal, a 12-foot-wide, grass-covered ditch, are in the foreground.

provides an introduction to the War of 1812 and a brief description of the battle of New Orleans. In addition there are displays of the many uniforms worn and the weapons used in the battle. (As of this writing, the second-floor exhibits were accessible only by a steep, winding staircase.)

A 1.5-mile road offers a clear view of the battlefield, with six markers explaining key events in the battle. Portions of the American defenses, including sections of the log barricade, and numerous cannons add to the site's sense of immediacy. A battlefield panorama gives the visitor a good view of what the British saw as they advanced. Park personnel provide detailed interpretive talks several times a day.

< 53 >

Location and Address Chalmette Unit, Jean Lafitte National Historical Park and Preserve, 8606 West St. Bernard Highway, Chalmette, LA 70043. Telephone: (504) 589-4430.

Operating Hours Open all year. May–October, daily 9:00 A.M.–6:00 P.M.; November–April, daily 9:00 A.M.–5:00 P.M.

Entrance Fees Admission is free.

Exhibits and Events Each year in January, Park Service personnel hold a three-day celebration of the battle of New Orleans. While the celebration is not an actual reenactment of the battle, volunteers are dressed in authentic uniforms. There are demonstrations of cannons, muskets, and rifles being fired. The specific dates in January for the three-day event vary from year to year.

Related Points of Interest

The Barataria Unit

Located ten miles south of New Orleans, this unit of Jean Lafitte National Historical Park and Preserve focuses on the rich plant and animal life of the bayous and swamps typical of the land through which the British force had to advance. A two-mile, self-guided walking tour provides visitors with a keen sense of the bayou region. It's difficult to imagine how the British managed to carry their heavy packs (each containing a cannon ball) and also drag their cannons through this terrain.

Location and Address The Barataria Unit, 7400 Highway 45 (Barataria Boulevard), Marrero, LA 70072. Telephone: (504) 589-2330.

Operating Hours Open all year. May–October, daily 9:00 A.M.–6:00 P.M.; November–April, daily 9:00 A.M.–5:00 P.M.

Entrance Fees Admission is free.

Jackson Square is at the edge of the French Quarter, near the Mississippi River.

Exhibits and Events In addition to viewing displays of the wildlife and animals of the bayou country, visitors can make reservations to take guided canoe trips through the bayous.

Jackson Square National Historic Landmark

This square, once called the Place d'Armes, is in the center of the French Quarter in New Orleans. In December 1803, the American flag was raised over the square for the first time, following President Thomas Jefferson's purchase of the Louisiana Territory from France. A flagpole in this tree-shaded park symbolizes the transfer of the Louisiana Territory to the United States. Andrew Jackson first reviewed his troops here and was honored by the people of the city after the battle.

Location and Address At the intersection of Decatur and St. Peter streets.

Horseshoe Bend National Military Park

Horseshoe Bend is a 100-acre peninsula formed by the Tallapoosa River. A three-mile road takes visitors through the site of the battle

< 55 >

of Horseshoe Bend, which took place on March 27, 1814, when Andrew Jackson led his Tennessee militia in an overwhelming victory over the Creek Red Sticks. The park actually covers more than 2,000 acres. The Visitor Center contains exhibits about Creek life, the life of frontier settlers, and the battle itself.

Location and Address Horseshoe Bend is located on the Tallapoosa River, in east-central Alabama, 12 miles north of Dadeville on State Route 49, approximately 94 miles southeast of Birmingham. Horseshoe Bend National Military Park, Box 103, Daviston, AL 36256. Telephone: (205) 234-7111.

Operating Hours Daily, 8:30 A.M.–5:00 P.M. Closed Christmas Day.

Entrance Fees Admission is free.

Exhibits and Events In mid-March each year park personnel and volunteers have a two-day encampment. People in the costumes

Named for the horseshoe-like curve of the Tallapoosa River, Horseshoe Bend was the site of a furious battle between Andrew Jackson's militia and the Creek Red Sticks.

< 56 >

and uniforms of the period demonstrate daily camp life (both among the militia and the Creek warriors), cannon firing, and the use of flintlock muskets. Park staff will also provide special demonstrations for school groups, if arrangements have been made in advance.

Fort McHenry National Monument and Historic Shrine

This famous star-shaped fort, built between 1798 and 1803, continued to function as an active military post until the end of World War II (1939–1945). It has since been restored to its pre-Civil War appearance in honor of the fort's survival of the British bombardment on September 12 and 13, 1814.

    Location and Address Fort McHenry is located about three miles from Baltimore Harbor, Exit 55 off I-95 to Key Highway, left

The American flag flies majestically over Fort McHenry, just as it did on the night Francis Scott Key wrote "The Star-Spangled Banner."

< 57 >

on Lawrence Street and left again on East Fort Avenue to the park entrance. Fort McHenry National Monument, Baltimore, MD 21230. Telephone: (410) 962-4290.

Operating Hours Daily, 8:00 A.M.–4:45 P.M. Closed Christmas Day and New Year's Day.

Entrance Fees $5.00 for adults; children under 16 are free.

Exhibits and Events At the Visitor Center, a 16-minute film on the battle of Baltimore and the writing of "The Star-Spangled Banner" is shown every half hour. Park personnel provide guided tours of the fort and grounds. During the summer months, the Fort McHenry Guard holds cannon-firing demonstrations, military drills, and flag-raising and lowering ceremonies. On Flag Day and Defenders' Day (the anniversary of the battle, held on September 12, 13, or 14), special programs are held which vary from year to year. Contact the Visitor Center for schedules and information.

The Hermitage National Historic Landmark

Andrew Jackson's plantation home is located about 12 miles east of Nashville, Tennessee. The residence, completed in 1819, is a storehouse of memorabilia from Jackson's adventure-filled life. The graves of both "Old Hickory" and his beloved wife, Rachel, are on the grounds.

Location and Address The Hermitage National Historic Landmark, also known as The Hermitage: Home of President Andrew Jackson, is located about 12 miles east of Nashville just off U.S. 70N. The Hermitage, 4580 Rachel's Lane, Hermitage, TN 37076-1344. Telephone: (615) 889-2941.

Operating Hours Daily, 9:00 A.M.–5:00 P.M. Closed Thanksgiving Day and Christmas Day.

Entrance Fees $8.00 for adults; $7.00 for seniors over 60; $4.00 for children ages 6–12; children under 6 enter free.

CHRONOLOGY OF THE WAR OF 1812

1803	The Napoleonic Wars begin in Europe.
1807	British ship *Leopard* fires on U.S.S. *Chesapeake*, killing 21 and impressing 4 sailors.
	"Free trade and sailors' rights" becomes a popular slogan.
1808	President Jefferson orders embargo on trade with Great Britain and France.
November 1811	American militia under William Henry Harrison defeat Tecumseh's warriors in the battle of Tippecanoe.
June 16, 1812	President Madison officially declares war against Great Britain.
August 1812	American ship *Constitution* defeats British *Guerrière*, gaining the nickname "Old Ironsides."
Autumn 1812	American forces unsuccessfully invade Canada—first from Detroit and later from the Niagara River and Lake Champlain.
1813	British Royal Navy blockades American coast.
September 1813	Captain Oliver Hazard Perry leads American naval force to victory in the battle of Lake Erie.
October 5, 1813	A U.S. force defeats British and Tecumseh and his braves in the battle of the Thames. Tecumseh is killed.
November 1813	Andrew Jackson leads Tennessee militia in first battles of the Creek War.
March 1814	Americans under Jackson defeat Creek Red Sticks in the battle of Horseshoe Bend.
April 1814	British defeat French and force Napoleon to step down as emperor.

< 59 >

August 24, 1814	British force invades Chesapeake Bay and sets much of Washington, D.C., ablaze.
September 11, 1814	Americans prevent a British invasion from Canada in the battle of Lake Champlain.
September 12, 1814	British make an unsuccessful attempt to take Mobile's Fort Bowyer from Jackson's defenders.
September 12–13, 1814	British bombardment of Baltimore's Fort McHenry fails. Francis Scott Key writes "The Star-Spangled Banner."
November 1814	Jackson invades Spanish Florida, British force flees, and Americans take Pensacola.
December 1, 1814	Jackson arrives in New Orleans.
December 8–14, 1814	British fleet arrives near Lake Borgne and defeats American gunboats on the lake.
	Federalists in New England hold anti-war Hartford Convention.
December 22–23, 1814	British force reaches Villeré plantation; Jackson leads surprise night attack that ends in a draw.
December 24, 1814	Major General Sir Edward Pakenham takes command of the British New Orleans force.
	Peace negotiators in Ghent, Belgium, sign the Treaty of Ghent, ending the war.
January 1, 1815	British and Americans wage a 3-hour artillery duel at New Orleans; American defenses are unharmed.
January 8, 1815	Final British assault on New Orleans is crushed by American artillery and rifle fire.
February 4, 1815	News of victory at New Orleans reaches Washington, D.C.
February 9, 1815	News of the peace treaty arrives in Washington, D.C.

FURTHER READING

Bosco, Peter I. *The War of 1812*. Brookfield, CT: Millbrook Press, 1991.

Dangerfield, George. *The Era of Good Feelings, 1814–1829*. New York: Ivan R. Dee, Inc., 1991.

Gay, Kathlyn, and Martin Gay. *War of 1812*. New York: Twenty-First Century Books, 1995.

Kroll, Paula. *By the Dawn's Early Light: The Story of the Star-Spangled Banner*. New York: Scholastic, 1994.

Morris, Neil. *The War of 1812*. Minneapolis, MN: Lerner Publications, 1985.

Steins, Richard. *A Nation is Born: Rebellion and Independence in America (1700–1820)*. New York: Twenty-First Century Books, 1993.

Whitcraft, Melissa. *Francis Scott Key*. Danbury, CT: Franklin Watts, 1994.

WEB SITES

Information about any historical park or battlefield landmark can be located by going first to:

http://www.NPS.gov/park//sts/index

A great resource for information on American History, including the battle of New Orleans, is:

http://www.thehistorynet.com

To find additional information on Jean Lafitte National Historical Park, go to:

http://www.nps.gov/jela

For a brief introduction to the War of 1812, go to:

http://www.multied.com/1812/

< 61 >

Information on the War of 1812, including its causes, major battles, and results, can be found at:

http://www2.andrews.edu/~downm/index.html

SOURCE NOTES

Part One

1. Quoted in Margaret L. Coit and the editors of *Life*, *Life History of the United States*, vol. 3, *The Growing Years, 1789–1829* (New York: Time, Inc., 1963), p. 97.

2. Quoted in Samuel Eliot Morison, *The Oxford History of the American People* (New York: Oxford University Press, 1965), p. 381.

3. Quoted in Robert M. Utley and Wilcomb E. Washburn, *The American Heritage History of the Indian Wars* (New York: Simon & Schuster, Inc., 1977), p. 133.

4. Ibid., p. 135.

5. Quoted in David C. King, et. al., *United States History* (Menlo Park, CA: Addison-Wesley Publishing Co., 1986), p. 172.

6. Quoted in Coit, *Life History*, p. 102.

7. Quoted in Richard B. Morris and Jane Woodress, eds., *Voices from America's Past*, vol. 1, *The Colonies and the New Nation* (New York: E. P. Dutton Co., 1963), p. 221.

8. Quoted in Page Smith, *A People's History of the Young Republic*, vol. 3, *The Shaping of America* (New York: McGraw-Hill Book Co., 1980), p. 634.

9. Ibid., p. 632.

10. Ibid., p. 641.

11. Ibid.

< 62 >

Part Two

1. Quoted in Reginald Horsman, *The War of 1812* (New York: Alfred A. Knopf, 1969), p. 227.

2. Quoted in Major James Ripley and Glenn Tucker, *The War of 1812: A Complete History* (New York: Hawthorn Books, 1969), p. 128.

3. Quoted in Robin Reilly, *The British at the Gates: The New Orleans Campaign in the War of 1812* (New York: G.P. Putnam's Sons, 1979), p. 197.

4. Quoted in Reilly, *The British at the Gates*, p. 101.

5. Quoted in Arthur M. Schlesinger, Jr., ed., *The Almanac of American History* (New York: Barnes & Noble Books, 1993), p. 220.

6. Quoted in Smith, *A People's History*, p. 648.

7. Quoted in Reilly, *The British at the Gates*, p. 227.

8. Quoted in Walter Lord, *The Dawn's Early Light* (New York: W. W. Norton and Co., 1972), p. 328.

9. Quoted in Morris and Woodress, *Voices From America's Past*, p. 225.

10. Quoted in Reilly, *The British at the Gates*, p. 210.

11. Quoted in Hugh Brogan, *The Penguin History of the United States* (New York: Penguin Books, 1990), p. 233.

12. Quoted in Lord, *The Dawn's Early Light*, p. 329.

13. Quoted in Morris and Woodress, *Voices From America's Past*, p. 226.

14. Quoted in Reilly, *The British at the Gates*, p. 274.

15. Ibid., p. 285.

16. Quoted in Lord, *The Dawn's Early Light*, p. 333.

17. Ibid., p. 335.

18. Quoted in Stuart A. Landry, *Side Lights on the Battle of New Orleans* (New Orleans: Louisiana Historical Society, 1965), p. 46.

19. Quoted in Reilly, *The British at the Gates*, p. 291.

20. Ibid., p. 290.

< 63 >

21. Quoted in Landry, *Side Lights*, p. 48.

22. Quoted in Lord, *The Dawn's Early Light*, p. 335.

23. Quoted in Reilly, *The British at the Gates*, p. 301.

24. Quoted in Lord, *The Dawn's Early Light*, p. 342.

25. Ibid., p. 343.

OTHER SOURCES

American Heritage, editors, *A Guide to America's Historic Places*. New York: American Heritage, 1985.

Berger, Josef, and Dorothy Berger, editors, *Diary of America*. New York: Simon & Schuster, 1957.

Boorstin, Daniel J. *The Americans: The National Experience*. New York: Random House, 1965.

Foner, Eric, and John A. Garraty, editors, *The Reader's Companion to American History*. Boston: Houghton Mifflin, 1991.

Stevens, Joseph E., *America's National Battlefield Parks*. Norman, OK: University of Oklahoma Press, 1990.

INDEX